RATTLE
OF THE
SUN

ISBN: 978-1-964003-23-8

Published by Decatur Dixon Press
Savannah, GA USA

Decatur Dixon Press champions emergent authors and artists whose work exists between genres, sharing interdisciplinary content that challenges traditional ideation, text, image, and structure.

Cover design by Jacob Edenfield
Book design by Jacob Edenfield
Printed in the United States of America

First Edition

Rattle of the Sun

Gregg Orifici

DECATUR DIXON PRESS

For Lynda, my dear friend and inspiration,
who lived voraciously and splendidly
and gave so many happy hours.

CONTENTS

FOREWORD ix

I.

CHATTERMARKS 3
STOIC 4
LATE BLOOMER 5
FLOWERS OF MY YOUTH 6
FLEURS D'AMBIVALENCE 8
GROWING UP 10
PEDALING THE AIR 11
WONDERING 12
DREAM 13
THE ICONIC POSTER OF FARRAH 16
OUR FATHER 17
RAVINE 18
THE WITCHING HOUR 19

II.

LET IT BE SAID 23
THE GARDENER 25
GOD SINGS TO ME IN FLOWERS 28
THE SECRET LIFE OF GARDENERS 29
BRAMBLING TO NEW QUAY 31
TABULA RASA 33
THE DEEP BREATH OF WINTER 34

III.

FROM PERINALDO 38
ECCOMIQUI 40

Mount Etna's Garden 43

My Side of the Palazzo 45

Pretense of Shelter 47

Garden of Entropy 48

Villa gallo 50

Palazzolo Acreide 52

This You Already Know 54

4,000 Miles Ago Yesterday 56

IV.

Homesteading 60

Life With an Artist 62

They Tried Divorce 63

Last Dial-Up Town in America 64

Incremental Darkening 67

Divulgence 68

Weltanschauung 69

After the Wall 71

Dubrovnik 1990 73

Irreconcilable Winters 74

V.

Amor Fati 79

Sunshine When it Snows 80

The Topography of Boca 83

Unsettled 85

Seek and You Shall Find 87

Interregnum 90

Wintermission 92

Here and Now 93

Confession 94

Still Standing 98

Denouement 100

FOREWORD

It is a joy to bring to life Gregg Orifici's first book of collected poems, *Rattle of the Sun*, and Decatur Dixon Press is honored to publish it as our very first original manuscript. His work shares something akin to the confidentiality of Ross Gay's poetry, the interchange between ache and everyday jubilance one feels in Ada Limón's poems, the presentness of the detail one loves in Mary Oliver, and an intimate sense of time's passage we encounter in the work of Mark Doty. What stands out most, to me perhaps, is the way that Orifici's words infuse even the heaviest weight with humor, a lightness of being that travels throughout the book.

Sauntering in late to the front row of a German language class, not long after the Fall of the Berlin Wall, Gregg, of indeterminate nationality, struck me like a visual poem unfolding. A poet-plantsman in the works, multilingual, a Long Islander with a southern drawl, he is a collector of character, from the floral to the fallible.

Rattle of the Sun, despite each day's intensities, declares "I am still standing." A favorite line uttered in the voice of a common weed: "I am Wildflower!" reminds me of its author, attuned to the exuberance of the everyday. This collection celebrates a shared human desire to stand up and shout, to *be*, and to outlast the deepest frost.

-Lisa Jaye Young

I.

CHATTERMARKS

Barchan drifts
race the sheep run
sculpting side chapel niches
where dwarf dunes
gambol snow quartz
glittering—

Inscrutable
altars to the woodland gods

      There
I deposit my triggers
my so-so serenity
well after well I empty
winter white every shade of blue—
howling
hushing, scattering

      I gather upon myself
what remains.

STOIC*

When the sky slumps
in winter
lumbering and fraught
I attune
to the scrape of the plow—
and the plowguy

Coatless sinew and scruff, cigarette
lips swamp maple sapling
bright eyed tired
well worn smile

I stoke the fire
first thing—
keep the kettle on,
biding my time

He keeps the truck running
while I sweeten his cup
I keep him talking,
smart-alecking,
my head flannelling,
deep in his passenger side

He's not in a hurry
never unkind
never mine—
                  still
I look for signs

for Ray White

Late Bloomer

Dahlias explode on the bridge
by the falls—late bloomers
who know there is little time
in October to beguile
with opalescence.

Short-lived seducers—
obscenely overpetaled
on spindly legs, saturated
in vermillion and gold
budding relentlessly
till frost bears down
        hard.

———

We picked them by the armful
knowing they weren't ours—
or long for this world.
We dropped our petals on your linoleum floor,
crushing them with bare feet
as we danced.

I threw you up in the air
with the Mamas and the Papas.
You landed in my arms, feathery.
Janis Joplin, Salomé, Oscar Wilde looked on,
held their breath, from the murals
that lined your walls. We collapsed
on your single bed, chest to chest,
petaled in sweat, spilling wine—

Unquenchable—and yet
        unavailable,
  for all that.

FLOWERS OF MY YOUTH

Today I wander
through the flowers of my youth

so few
I can hardly forget
the bougainvillea
its papery red
so veined—
I felt myself
exposed
from the inside,
raw and beating

the shock of cotton candy
outside my window
double handfuls
of pink so pink
the Kwanzan cherry
bouqueted me
petaling my pillow, my blankets,
pinking my dreams

———

I was a sensitive boy
like the mimosa
whose leaves curled
to my touch
in the dry back corner of our yard
where no one noticed
me climbing up
into a dizzying happiness
of another world
       so fragrant
I could barely hold on

———

as for fruit there was none
in my childhood
apart from cellophane roll-ups and
the cryo glare of the grocery aisle—

who knew that fruit came from flowers
in the suburban seventies?—

the maelstrom
where science meets slang
and slang meets your mother.

Fleurs d'Ambivalence

monstera deliciosa or
philodendendron bipinnatifidum?

we had one
or the other
in the chocolate shag of my childhood—
the living room we hardly used
except to play Burt Bacharach or *My Fair Lady*
on the black lacquer record player console or
on Tuesdays after school when Frau Teufel would light
her cigarette in a slim silver holder and hover
over me at the matching black piano—her bony oily
virtuoso fingers grasping my plump quibbling ones on the keys
as if she could will them into submission
straight to a concert *Halle*—
exhaling smoke rings that would waft in my face
chanting root chord root chord in a black and white voice
that made me sit up straight

I stuck with the Teufel for my mother
who said I'd be the life of the party,
that I'd regret quitting—I told her
I couldn't breathe

the *monstera deliciosa* or whatever it was
constantly drinking in its white stylish planter
beckoned me with brawny green hands
growing so big so fast they distracted me
from the piano and threatened to take down
the smokey chrome lamp from Bloomingdale's Clearance
arching across the room, shag to ceiling

I used to think my *monstera*—
also called a Swiss cheese tree,
its massive foliage gaping with holes,

was my beanstalk to the future—
if it would grow to seventy feet, its maximum height,
Swiss cheese might escape through the roof
and set a boy free

————

Swiss was our family favorite
growing up—individually wrapped in plastic
like American, its only cheese competition
Teufel too was Swiss
she said
but I was not curious   back then
who knew about cheese
or could tell
one German accent from another—
        I just scrubbed my hands
        open-windowed the air
and life
        and the occasional party
eventually
found me.

GROWING UP

Admittedly, they probably weren't
Abbott and Costello squeezing through
our tiny, second story window,
but who else could they be?
For hours, I tracked their progress
as they walked right out of the moon,
slow and steady onto our street—
please God, go somewhere else,
please—
then, boingo—
there they were
parting our Flintstones curtains.

At any time, I could have pulled
my brother's leg hanging
from the bunk above, or screamed
for my parents. Maybe I thought
I was invisible deep in the shadow.

It got so loud in my head it felt airless,
even with November pouring in.
Closer and closer they came, and closer still,
feeling for me, as if their only sense
was smell, highly tuned—
to me.

When their heads completely eclipsed
the moon, I could see their pouting mouths
and unblinking judgement—
I put a hand to my own mouth
to cut off my essence.

PEDALING THE AIR

Fireballs and candy buttons
face flush with freedom—
who loves the world
more than a boy riding his Big Wheel
two whole blocks to the park?

Revving past
the fire engine playground
the duck pond's honk and scream—the surprise
of being lifted up
by the collar
        by some kid's older brother
held aloft
pedaling the air
       biting my tongue
as my first love   rode away
big bully at the wheel.

WONDERING

She stared at me nightly
Across seven seasons
Of cut-out, taped-up NY Mets yearbooks—
Ballplayers and batting averages spanning
An entire wall—along with Farrah, her pinup competition.

She was a different kind of beautiful. I loved her
In a denim shirt tied at the waist—
She was more than she appeared.

Wonder Woman made people speak
The truth. She golden-lassoed them.

I half hoped she'd lasso *me*—
Tired of half-truths and hiding.

But she was Wonder because she *could* hide.
She had a getaway plane to make her invisible—
Plus her street-chic human disguise.

While I wandered away from the world—
Its playgrounds and barbed-wire—she twirled
And shazammed into a warrior princess of peace.
Bulletproof bracelets, kickass boots,
star-spangled chic.

I could only dream—

And wonder. What made her different made her strong.
She fought back when she had to. Fitting in isn't everything.
Most people wouldn't notice
A boy gulping down his fear.

Everyone has a superpower, Wonder taught me—
What was mine?

DREAM

I
cross-
slap my arms
out from my chest
scrunch my eyes whiplash
my non-existent ponytail
and pray for magic—
when just about
any change
will do

I saw her
only in reruns
but still I dream of Jeannie

———

Cursed
shrunk stuck
in a bottle
She loves him
so handsome so lost so
human

Delirious
she pinks
and comes out swirling
No more bumping against glass walls glass floor
glass-stoppered ceiling
Free at last to cross her arms
and blink and be
who she's meant to be

Her gift is strong
but he wishes only one simple thing—
not even the standard three
He does not care
what else she can do,
is not curious
about her experience or her desires,
does not embrace her
He worries
what people think

Hers is not an everyday kind
of love, she knows
She knows

What he wants
is Normal
so with all her willpower
she blinks herself back in the bottle
(what she won't do for love)
and waits—
impatiently
in limbo for how long?

——

I was born the year
Jeannie emerged granting wishes—
Bottled up and pretending
I dreamed of her
when the first man I loved
went back to his girlfriend and the next
found my cooking too crude—
and no amount of wishing
or waiting or
reconstituting
would change a thing

Still—
an occasional
Jeannie gesture
pink and perfectly executed—
would you blame me?

The Iconic Poster of Farrah *

Her hair lies in wait like a lion,
it curls and waves and pounces—
sighs winningly, absentmindedly
caressing her swimsuit which seems
too shy to be red—not wanting to show
even an inch of midriff, a peek
of breast, no cleavage, just
one slightly erect nipple calling attention
to itself—irritated perhaps by the cool
lycra, not trying to be provocative,
or intrude.

What happened to all the Farrah boys—
whose teenage walls and closet doors
she transfigured? Her pin-up smile, and wile,
corroborated us—strained and unreadable
as our desire. Her hair, the world's most teased
and fabulous, offered sanctuary—
even as it mocked
our own feeble camouflage. What
would we not have given
to have had a skateboard stunt double, too?

It couldn't be easy—all that smiling
(20 million sold!), even in LA
at the cusp of stardom, an Angel in the making.
I am tired, she confides. I don't
feel glamorous.

She wants what you want but
can barely imagine;
You must change your life.

*in homage to Rilke

OUR FATHER

Who art, I pray,
now in heaven—
you stepped out on us.

Restless and shallow-rooted,
flush with corny charms
and undisclosed reserves,
you traded us in
        our wood-paneled station wagon
for a two-seater convertible—
the other woman
gold-necklaced you #1—
and that was all
it took.

We were teenage captives
to your bikini-clad stewardess—
bluegreen eyeshadow,
overcurled hair, lips pursed and pouting.
Driving, you'd pore over her photos
pressed up against the windshield—
daring us to look, or disapprove.

What sorry looked like
you never mastered.

Were you happy? Or
was it all bluff and swagger—
We weren't angels, we
cold-shouldered, we took sides.
We just wanted what we had—

        You wanted different.

Ravine

Don't look down
I beg you
on the twisted road from Dolceacqua—
yet of course you must
to admire the concentric circles of Apricale,
content and swirling in the valley below.
Look past the ravine of discarded microwaves,
vanities that have lost their allure,
and the occasional Fiat, flipped, crushed,
ass in the air—exhausted, perhaps
switchbacking
light into shadow, shadow then light,
making painfully slow progress
until—
spent   or
uncurbed by resolve,
one cuts a corner
and heads straight down

Love
can turn out
like this.

The Witching Hour

It was an orange creamsicle evening—
Wisping clouds catch swirls
of color.   Heat
slackens its grip
on the day.

The wind picks up a sweater chill. What
light remains, slanted, softening, invites you to look
right at the sun, yoked low on the horizon. The witching hour,
as always, begins with birds seeking cover, twirling their wonderments
and furthermores. And when the frogs join in
their baritone throating meets the singsong soprano from the trees
in a fleeting chorus—an everyday finale
that reminds you the end is near
and you—
    are very much alive.

II.

LET IT BE SAID

I am Solidago
but my admirers—alas more in Europe
than here at home—call me Goldenrod.
Yes I grow along roadsides and
in every open field, but *I* am *not* a weed—

I am Wildflower.

And native. There are 120 branches
on my family tree—in North America alone.
We are Firecrackers! Every one of us. The last must-attend party
of summer, we herald the Big Change with our many golden banners,
finely woven, undeniably opulent, waving in the wind to greet you—
and every type of pollinator—

I give you—Yellow!

And yet some of you—I won't name names
but to shame!— call me Weed.

I am Pollinator Magnet.

Thank god I am prolific, what otherwise would they do—
the native honeybees, moths, butterflies,
beetles, beneficial wasps, leaf-hoppers—shall I go *on*?

I hope you do not have me confused with my Nemesis!

Ragweed, problem child, ridiculously named
Ambrosia, with insignificant flowers,
more green than lustrous yellow, unfit for a ditch, let
alone the bouquet. He not me—
his airy-fairy pollen, not mine, which is crafted and
solid—think specially tailored, rather than, well, just
blowing everywhere with the wind—serves only himself,

overcrowding the air with allergens
and *mishegas*.

Your sneezing has nothing, let me repeat, NOTHING
to do with me.

Have you seen me and my lovely sisters gathering for a sway
in the neighbor's meadow? We are a sight to behold! When at last
you get over your prejudice, that anything growing in abundance
is an infestation, you'll be left gasping—
in awe, of course, not hay fever—

You are Privileged— if I do say so myself—
to be part of a world so well-endowed, so rich,
it is carpeted, as far as any eye can see, in the most precious,
life-giving, soul-soothing,
soaring—gold.

THE GARDENER*

She built her dream
On a south facing slope
A perennial wonderland
High Halifax had never seen—
Dig and divide, share-the-wealth Mother
Superior, sacred source
Of every erstwhile garden and gardener
In all the hilltop domains

————

We met in winter
On the neighbor's pond—
Timeless toe loops and legs
Perfectly perpendicular, not
Ninety pounds with her skates on.
White-water racer, backcountry guide
She knew my one rhododendron, and scraggly phlox,
She figure-eighted me, whispering
Come by in the spring.

So

After the snows
And the mud
Swamp maples and peepers,
I show up
To dozens of lunch bags of soil and shoots
Just breaking through
Tagged in latin and common, water and sun,
I've been waiting for you

Walks and talks
Year after year, flood after freeze,
I harvest botanical cheat sheets and baggies, and reread
Her June fairytale of marsh marigold and

Primrose in opera house tiers, dipping their toes
In artfully dammed pools, hellebores, astilbe
A scramble of streams.

She enlists me
In her campaign
To grow the blue Himalayan poppy.
Shares her seed and her sadness
When her decades-old carpet
Of heath and heather, calluna and ericaceae
Turned threadbare in successive
Snowless winters.

———

She visits me at a civilized hour—
Eighty something, crowned in straw, silver braid
Rapunzelling to the waist, wellies and
Long sleeves for the flies—
To tour my far-flung beds and borders
Filled with her progeny.

Artemisia and saxifrage, a shade of pink
Too demanding, brush piles critters
And compost, bards and barred owls
Pollinators in decline—

Socratic musings and companiable silence,
Climate change and soil ph—

Oh, the thrill of finding a wildflower
Or lungwort, whose silver spots
Catch her eye.
When she accepts a shovel
Of each for her garden, she turns my world
Upside down.

———

It's more work, her world without mulch—
The daily bend and fall to knee,
Constricted fingers and forearms, mindless hours

Weeding out the unwanted. But there are gifts.
Nature's whimsical, self-sowing splatter—
Unexpected treasure, extravagant bounty
And the greatest of all—giving it all away.

Lupin, daylilies, elecampane—
Imperialists
She banishes to the roadside—or where
Her husband can restrain them
With the mower
Myrrhis odorata, Sweet Cicely, white lace
On sugary stems, she keeps to herself,
Despite my pleadings
And pizzelles.

Not well behaved
My child, my Cicely runs wild—
The bully on the playground
Only a mother could love.

* for Elizabeth Hull

GOD SINGS TO ME IN FLOWERS

it must be God
the all-animator
who speaks to me in flowers—
from a righteous bed
of many-petaled peonies
singing
shouting in my face
        you are not the star
        you think you are

bluebells pulsing
chanting
        yes! yes!
in my wooded head

pulmonaria
hums in my chest
soothing me saturating
and I
forget myself
completely
when at last I hear the primrose
giggle

        lo! lo!
the redeeming truth
of the pawpaw's moan
Sarah Vaughn
Nina Simone
and I know

the taste of the fruit
to come.

THE SECRET LIFE OF GARDENERS

I do not tread lightly
in this garden—fragile beauty I crush
and cleave
as I make my way—
I am Gardener
and like all my people, mercurial in manner—
gentle earthchild, smelling like the rose, *and* imperious diva,
yanking out plants roots and all, or lacerating them at the knee and
elbow—
torturing the too tall, too thick, the too lush and the can't keep up.

I eradicate the masses
distracting to the eye—my eye—
to showcase the most magnificent by eliminating the runners up,
cutting off food production capacity, defeating their exuberance—

All for an illusive state of balance, of resplendence, that, I confess,
I may see differently the next day, or moment.

Perhaps the plant's only sin was to grow faster than its neighbor,
or bloom at the wrong height, or time—blurring the intricate tapestry
woven only in my head. Alas, its penance may be
the hobbling of its limbs in prime.

Understand—
being ruthless isn't easy—
Playing God in the garden is not a job, it's perennial
purgatory—and a calling.
People praise my work ethic, my vision—
So successful am I in my garden tyranny, I am celebrated
on two continents—
except by my mostly defenseless subjects
who cannot get out of the way.

What must they think when they see me coming

brandishing my deadly arsenal—clippers,
trowel, slayer, and saw?
      They should be quaking in their roots.

———

I do not sing to them or whisper kind words
so they may flourish. I suffer them
no false sympathy, I do not condescend—
They know who I am
      and what I am capable of.

My mutterings are but convenient apology. I prune first,
ask forgiveness never.

Mine is not the work of survival,
it's the opposite of that.

I love what I do—
God help me.

BRAMBLING TO NEW QUAY

on the cliffs along the gray green sea
Dylan Thomas walks before me

there are sheep of course
the grazing fields as evening falls
all the world
it seems pulses
tawny brown and ochre

the path twiddles
round rocky coves and headlands
my thoughts speckle   blown
as they are by the wind offshore
out of reach

strange as it seems I hardly notice
the burn on my shins and ankles—
my forearms push through
the blue black crowding

only when I see myself skinless
scalpelled red and darker dripping
only then do I notice
the thorny brambles and
berries shrieking
to be picked—

I oblige

some so sour my body shudders
others so ripe I taste the onset
of decay
my hands my face so bruised
with berry
that a man squeezing past
aghast

admonishes me
to leave a few for the birds
        I do my best

but I am flogged
by the canes I've uprooted—
beauty over bounty—in my own garden—
careless days
of sweetness trod to dirt
untasted

———

here now the setting sun
with the coming of the tide
my heart stumbles there is blood on my hands
and mouth coppery
salt on sugar—
I gorge
jam full my sack
and know
it will never be the same

tomorrow
I leave this place
in awe of this splendor this life
no longer young I fear
I will not get my fill
hunger suckers me staggering
I race against the gloom spitting seeds
no longer able
to tell rancid from unready
no longer mattering
I

do not go softly into that good night...
I rage, rage against the dying of the light

Tabula Rasa

after the staggering storm
      the hewing   the undoing
I am not
the man
I used to be

I am
what I always was
        becoming

The Deep Breath of Winter

White blind, lashes frozen
top to bottom.
Throat cold-knifed, silenced.
Chafed and chored by existence.

Gone, moonlight's shawl of surrender,
morning's humbling embrace.
Each day a consolation, a balm—
repairs of a season yet to come.

We are lost to each other—
disembodied fires flaring between drafts
of forgiveness. The traverse is treacherous
wood pile to stove,

your bed to mine.
We flurry about, jittery
snow squalling, deepening—
questions piling up, precarious
the accumulation.

Some winters are like this.

III.

FROM PERINALDO

It's a quarter to seven. From my terrace I see Monte Alto,
Giardino and Torragio blush with the rising sun.
I look down at medieval Apricale, its swirling streets still in shadow,
and Ventimiglia, at the mouth of the Nervia, where they just had a scare.
The Mediterranean floods the horizon, sheds its gray veil
for the royal blue it knows we prefer. Word is that San Remo,
five miles east, home to a Beaux Arts casino designed by Ferret,
now has two cases. It's February's end. 2020.

The vacation it seems is over. I'm alone
in a friend's hilltop tower, and I can hear the alarm bells ringing.
I'm not deaf to the world's sickness and fear,
even with my mediocre Italian.

No radio, no wifi; the TV I tried to figure out, but it's complicated
and German. I ask the vegetable seller what she thinks, the bartender,
on whom I have a crush—how many new cases,
how close, how many dead. For the umpteenth time,
I ask myself if now is the time. To go. I hear from a hiker
on the trail to Bordighera, that they're thermal-sensing the trains,
quarantining anyone with the slightest temperature,
along with everyone else in the car. Public buildings, museums—
all closed. The post office won't let people in. I had to buy stamps
through a crack in a boot-blocked door. Churches are padlocked.
Self-confessions only.

I horde all this, arrange and rearrange the pieces,
inert in a stalemate of indecision.
It's off season and I am growing out my hair—what's left of it—
my latest vanity. I see almost no one. It's March now,
shutters are strapped. Locals have bolted,
waiting for summer—or normalcy—to return.
I read Pasolini, Cavalli
and write poems no one will read,
then, when I have exhausted all the color from the sky,

and welcomed back Venus, I descend three stories
to prepare the pasta and artichokes I bought in Venti—
before the scare—and ration the wine. Not
that there's any shortage, not yet, but it feels
decadent, dulling my senses in a tightrope time.

From Perinaldo, it seems the world is dozing.
Last night strong winds knocked over three potted lemons
while last-minute flights out of Europe are tripling
and my stomach is somersaulting. As if
a war is brewing and I need to catch
what may be the last ride out—I just don't know how,
or where it's safe to go.

There's a bar in Dolceaqua with wifi a steep two hours away.
Last time I WhatsApp'd David from there,
Donna Summer's *Hot Stuff* was playing so loud
I could barely hear his concern.

From the trail, if it's clear, I'll be able to see France, my way out,
and, hopefully, trains still crossing the border. I'll buy a newspaper
I'll spend the afternoon translating, which may ummph me to action.
Staggering nowhere,
I'll stock up on oranges, for the vitamin C, and grappa,
my makeshift hand-sanitizer, even though they'll weigh me down
on my trek back to the tower.

My thoughts flutter like cards in a slow shuffle. I'm stupored,
terracotta-baked and affixed to my terrace.
I smell pine and eucalyptus,
and the gas furnace. The sky turns acid orange
above the Alps to the west,
then mauve, and finally darkens. Who knows
how long till I follow the sun.

Eccomiqui

Here I am
getting-on gardener
wintering—in the Vermont sense—
in a *palazzo* garden in Sicily—
thrilled to be raking and weeding
around hundreds of prickly plants and cacti,
pickaxing miraculous infestations
of oxalis and gladioli
any New England gardener would kill for
and planting giant agave and Bismarck palms
xanthorrhoea australis and the more mundane—
dahlia zinnia *basilico* in line
with ten types of tomato— in soil
that is practically lava

Three sweet *giardinieri*
and I (for a time)
maintain the *marchesi's* gardens
somersaulting it seems to keep on top of the leaves
pulito pulito then epic winds and sandstorms
from the Sahara—
and guests!

In the garden
irrigation is art
Arab engineering and muscle
turning rusty valves
of ancient *vasque* channeling
cool water from *saja* to fountain
safariing through garden rooms
pergolas orchards and *pratos*
until *ovviamente*
something breaks down
and three plastic watering cans
two with not insignificant leaks

must be fetched
to keep a thousand priceless plants
from withering
in the unrelenting sun

We understand each other
my *giardinieri coleggi* and I
about seventy *percento*
I'm not sure if it's Sicilian
or slang or the sweaty grunting of gardeners
but it seems they swallow the jiggly end
of every word   so

I try it out—verbs without endings,
garbling without grammar—
and *va bene cosi*

we fling friendly insults
and smalltalk
as we hoe under poppies
so thick it could be Oz—I could be
one of the guys, I think, the *ragazzi*—until
somebody says something incomprehensible
and I stand there   uprooted

———

a month later my man
my *gran artista*
brings over his paints and pencils from America
and plants himself in the garden
he sweettooths my gardeners
every week with *cornetti alla crema*
smiles ooze
when they see their own portraits on the packaging
they fight over the chocolate the vanilla and
who's pictured
strongarming the wheelbarrow?
wielding the *zapa*...
who is the *più bello?*

one of gardeners, the most dramatic,
says he will cry like the sky
next month when we leave—
I search my Sicilian
I'm seventy percent sure
he isn't talking about the rainy season to come.

MOUNT ETNA'S GARDEN

Etna *montana*
Dama vulcana
      she speaks to me
in the garden

at times she wears her fresh white veil
or shy for days she forges
rare rings of love
that marry her to this fertile land
where again and again
she empties her womb

non disturbarmi
she tells me as I lay down my *zapa*
do not disturb
the fecund earth the soil of my inside
is alive—but only
underneath—
the world you cannot see

so let it be she says
non disturbarmi
I do not wish the secrets of my soul
uncovered

———

what we call weeds
are her *bella famiglia*
the poppies that scatter their seed
let them live
she bellows
glory to the gladioli—
warriors spearing through lava,
Etna's many painted fingers—
Admire me!

there is a place where
giant fennel and scabiosa
oxalis and Queen Anne's lace
dance circles
around ancient *olive*
and *pompelmi rossi*—

and *Dama vulcana* knows
that place
should not be whacked
and mowed
like a crabgrass *prato*

it disturbs her sleep
it fumes her—
so *per favore*
non disturbarmi
she implores
it makes my belly ache—
and rumble

MY SIDE OF THE PALAZZO

out of sight
marchesi courtyard
chiesa bougainvillea
and *sì*, the secrets
of the *giardino Arabo*
lush and *aromatico*

my side
of the *palazzo*
past the kitchens
the laundry
ancient storerooms of
> *vino*
> *olio di olive*
> *marmelada*

beyond
a recording studio on delay
Mick Jagger's I'll be back some day

my side of the palace
the quiet side
afternoons when the sun bares down
tractors weed wackers and wheelbarrows still
there is nothing left then
to excavate
or water
the *camponnone*, its
overtaxed espresso machine
the working man's heart and hive
deserted now
> *pranzo*
> *siesta*
> *famiglia*

only then
after my pickaxing

and barrowing is done
only then   do I *caffe latte*
or *negroni*
on my staircase landing
sunsetting ancient olives and not so
ancient Villasmundo
powerlines and palm trees and hovering
old Etna   her smoker's cough
and rings bedazzling.

Pretense of Shelter

simpering
midday heat
when even lizards seek the shade
of spontaneous snapdragons
or burrow
into unknowable crevices
          as we do
slithering into the café
its cavernous cool

too tempting
the fuchsia *terrazzo*
it's half-assed awning
sun slipping through the canes
          inescapable
the shout and revv of the *strada*

all Modica—the people the dogs
the saints—pouring down the steep steps
of the *Duomo*, like rain seeking stasis
pooling and purifying, yearning
          for home

GARDEN OF ENTROPY

From a derelict rooftop
on the new town side of the Old Spanish Gate, we look out
over Sicily's *Megara Hyblaea*, once a pulsing Greek colony,
now overlooked Augusta. What we see
is remarkable—a fleet of battleships and a ship graveyard, belching
orange petrochemical sprawl, epochs of church spires,
and one extremely loud dredging machine, birds shrieking,
flamingos flying off for quieter shallows.

The 12th century Swabian castle that hovers over us,
long since a jail, was abandoned in the eighties,
after a prisoner breakout. Trees grow in and out of windows
and over its many roofs. Huge blocks of crenellation tumble
onto jutting terraces, cluttering a nearby park, and gather
in massive heaps at the edge of the sea.

Impossible to leave—

We perch on cushions of capers and wild asparagus seeding
a crumbling rampart lichened in a peach-orange
I've never seen. It splotches perfectly with the spray paint graffiti
on the walls that surround us. Of course, there is plastic everywhere,
of every color—

So much color, it blurs

Tutti frutti snapdragons growing in cracks,
striped blue thistle, scrubby pink lilacs, a purple vine—
some cross of petunia and morning glory—insinuating itself
everywhere, red red valerian, and spent blooms in inky cobalt
puddled in the crevices. With all this,
and the graffiti and the trash, we are caught
by strips of cloth and tape, in amazing fluorescence,
whipping in the wind—shuddering,
heraldic flags of the *castello*.

We bask in the anarchy

Leaning against thick black piping and split white energy conduits.
Wires, splayed in bouquets, slip across the ancient stones
or catapult themselves over the spray-painted walls. As did *Ale,*
oversweet, appearing from nowhere, half-toothed, carrying
his portfolio of penciled kitties, that he earnestly
shares. We hunker down
on a fallen chunk of castle, nowhere in particular to go—

Self-seeders in a garden of entropy
colonizing the sun.

Villa Gallo

Billowing, acid-yellow swells
marry wilding courtyards
to roofless outbuildings, fallen terracotta tiles
two-feet deep
cover the ground where once
they covered indispensable tools,
crates of oranges, barrels of olive and wine—

      sparkings of time

Charred remnants of rafters splinter the roof piles
like enormous black chopsticks
thrown down helterskelter as the flames took hold.
Just outside, formidable, burnt sculptures of armed prickly pear
guard the wreckage—

      what phoenix would ever rise here?

We make plaintive foot music surveying the accumulation,
broken tiles clamoring—a xylophone interpreting
the remains, our boots for mallets.

Near and far, possibly still salvageable villas
and storehouses stilled
by slap-dash windbreaks are fed
by galloping strands of crumbling aqueducts,
braceleted by stone arches and
now-contorted wrought iron, dressed
in faded coats of arms, vestiges of gold—

Remnants, these, of a story centuries old
when ample water and workers
blushed this land with bounty—

      a fairy tale—or its flipside

This, the relics
of the tyranny of the sun,
is the world of bees—

Brash, drunk on yellow, like the view
that greets us from the ruin's high porcupine splatter—
        pastoral
phlegmatic waves of florescence
rippling across fields to the next hill, the next heap
of history, up the slopes of towering,
twitchy Mt. Etna—

Blurred to the east, a scent of sea, Calabria rising—
bare knuckles paling,
like the present, mist into mist.

PALAZZOLO ACREIDE

They roar into the piazza
like a flock of swifts, not-unwelcome
invaders—circling and revving, striped
in green orange pink fluorescence,
not inclined to cut their engines, rather to strut
their gleaming bikes preening helmets tapered leathers,
sluicing the air, creating a wind funnel
swirling the baroque Piazza del Popolo
pulling everything—even towering *San Sebastiano*—
with magnetic muscle to their orbit.

The leader slows to a stop at *Caffe Sicilia,*
and the flock takes over the terrace where I sit. They surround me
suits unzipped to the waist, helmets pedestalled on chairs and tables
like sculpture, they stretch and itch and carouse
beers and olives in the midday sun, newly colonizing the old world
on their way to who knows where. I am open-mouthed
by their brilliance, the smell of their sweat and warm leather, the smile
of a rapturous, leonine man that catches me
enroute to a fellow biker—begetting a blush
and the dream of hopping on
and holding tight.

One of the younger Rotarians
(embroidered wagon wheels one and all)
is Roman marble brought to life—rosey fulvous skin,
ginger beard, dark scattered curls plastered
in a helmet wave, and milky deep set eyes so alluring
they could be mascara'd. A sweet soldier
with blood-red knee and elbow pads protruding
his cyclesuit, a perfect padded motorman ass
and take-no-prisoners Forma boots that look as if
they contain jetpacks—or could conquer the moon. He stands vaping
among similar riders, each with their own flair, a red bandana
around the neck, a leather flame burning up a thigh—

Some of the men are older, comradely lines inscribed on their foreheads,
skin hardened by wind and sun, hair woven with gray—
one stands out in blue jeans, tight fitting,
and Doc Marten boots. He's patting the backs of other men, rubbing
their shoulders, while sweettalking the one woman rider across the
terrace into joining their table.

Much older men, with colorful canes and walkers,
occupy the tables at the edges in the shade,
cackling with their younger dreams. Beautiful *bambini*
and teens wheelie in front of us, brandishing
blinding new mountain bikes, eager for the day
they can upgrade.

The gang, caught up
in the business of being, ups the volume,
after the roaring silence of the road.
They are raveled, whole,
holding each other up, arms
around shoulders, around waists—a firm grip
where they belong, and to whom—
nothing to grudge,
or hold back.

I close my eyes—
there's no rushing the sun.

This you already know

Scicli in the shade
of a closed café
the chairs empty now
but oh *ieri sera* spritzes and black sweaters,
bright lights on the amphitheater cliffs, the ruins, the *castello*
Piazza del Carmine, the center of the universe—
baroque splendor, staircased streets, full-bodied *Nero d'Avola*,
a stage set of moonlight music and big flocks of teens,
why you came here to Sicily   why
you were born—

———

My ancestors, it seems, surrendered too soon.
Impatient with lava, *non c'e' lavoro*,
earthquakes, failed harvests, homes abandoned,
the mafia *forse*—who knows
why the story of America sold so well—
everyone had an uncle, a cousin—not a word came back
unvarnished, just *lire* for steerage, 3 months at sea—
unimaginable
slums in paradise, its homegrown unwelcome.

My kin left Sicily
worn out and crumbling, never dreaming
their backwater would bounce back,
that joy would return,
tourists would come,
then too many—

There must be grumbling in heaven—

———

I don't know
which chair to take,
which view, there the statue the fountain,

that way the river—
I pine for this, my birthright
that tomorrow I too must abandon,
who knows when to return.

I get why they left—
what for
the fullness of history
when your stomach is hollow
and hope caught a boat?

When you look around
and see only the past—it doesn't matter
whether you dig in or move on—
This, is where homesick begins.

4,000 MILES AGO YESTERDAY

Gone Catania
chittering lights
on Etna's broad shoulder
gone *marchesi's* noble palazzo
swaddled
in bougainvillea and fig—
          Home now
to Vermont's silent
star-smeared skies—
the only crowd around

4,000 miles ago yesterday
captive to Sicily's howling
windswept nights
we walked marble pathways
Persian-patterned
through palms aligned
to Etna's who-knows-when caldera—
gnarled olives
shaded us on Bellini benches sweetened
by jasmine, littered with spilled fruit—
          a dreamlife
I remember only
when breathing

At times the sounds I hear
ring true to dream but
now they're our dogs—four
querulous creatures
barking barking
part-Sicilian in their pen—
and the mowers and skidders
of our own dirt world—
the whizz and whirl
of Vermont in season

my daily scutterings
now
through wondrous green
shrubby pinks and purple
perennials
here there
and everywhere I plant
as if I too
the *marchesi*

———

No longer do I scramble
to beg or sneak the Panda farm car
through the ancient gate
no more baroque over-the-top
blurring my eyeballs,
the chased-down Caravaggio
behind me now
as I grab my own scuffed Subaru
crammed with pluffy peonies and bendy canopies
of too-tall trees circling my windshield
hollyhocks hugging the gear shift
soil spilling
stalks cracking
stop and go no
looking back or
right—so slowly
I scramble on
       neck swerved
black flies swirling
splattering
like lava
disappearing
smoke rings and sunshine
perennial sparkings
there then
and here
       now

IV.

HOMESTEADING

Whoever once homed the brick house—
now falling in on itself, overgrown and gaping
on a dirt track above a dammed river—
I am sitting on your sofa.

Chippendale, we *think*—but
why leave those bolts of damask—oddly colored,
not orange, not quite brown—in your surprisingly dry,
almost roofless attic? Your fabric now curtains our living room.
Another bolt, wispy greens on taupe, slipcovers the sofa.

We drink morning coffee from your hand-painted mugs
(was it your hand?), and wipe our mouths
on blue Irish linen we ripped from its original packing.
Your infestation—your books, your decades
of *National Geographic* and *Paris Match*—quilled by porcupines,
scatted, torn—
has resettled itself
on our shelves and floorboards.

———

Your rot became a must-see derring-do
for friends from afar—
scaling piles of an accumulated lifetime, shimmying
staircases without stairs, spelunking
your darkest cavities, excavating fur coats *and*
furry creatures, still-coated, half hibernating.

Our friends too helped themselves
to your progeny—precious catkins
scattered by a profligate wind.

What happened? Were you the last
of your kind?
Did you go mad
from hoarding? Will we?

Madame Violette DuBois we named you
for the blue flowers that pucker your foundation
and carpet the woodland edge
fast approaching.

The framed Sacred Heart we found tossed
or tumbled in a tangle of sumac
and winterberry
was cracked and starting to mold.
There too, a rusty shovel—a sign.

We dug up the winterberry
and liberated Jesus.
We brought him home—a charm.

A pardon, perhaps
                    a reprieve.

LIFE WITH AN ARTIST

The hills flex
their biceps over Fort Morrison valley,
strong arming the impastoed pastures
through which I speed from you daily
and return.

Stooped over my inbox,
I can see the cut of the powerlines
where you park your truck by the North River
day by day painting the trapeze of ridges
abstracting the sky.

Your vision lines gallery walls
and every flat surface of our lives.

Days where past is present and future
tightens its grip— those days end
passed out on the kitchen floor,
dinner a cold thought in the fridge.

Cricketsong at dusk, mothballed
jackets, a bed full of doghair.
A perfect flat stone gleaned
from a ruin. The old red globe lantern
sunsetting our center hall.

If I am patient, the paint
that never washes off your hands
colors the places you touch me.
Or you turn stormy. Unpredictable
Irish sky. A lone bull in the field.

I am that curve in the road
you never manage to paint.

THEY TRIED DIVORCE

but it didn't take.
They divided dinnerware
and sofas, peonies and bittersweet—
then the moving truck came and went. Still

they circled back—soil too sweet, perhaps

or too rocky—to uproot them.
For years they dug each other up—
wheelbarrowed and crowbarred
the possibilities

then heeled each other back in, relieved,
re-rooting—

Their particular glue: dreams
of the garden tour,
a puritan grit,
and, of course, tradition

Neither set of parents
gave up their own fight. They just held on
and on, white knuckles on the dinner table,
the church pew, the carpool steering wheel—

      More than indifference
      more than a tolerance for pain—
perhaps in the long run
      inertia was to blame.

Last Dial-Up Town in America

I.

Saul Bellow hid out here for decades.
Elisha Otis, and thus the elevator, were native sons.
Boom town in the early '80s. Tanneries,
Mills and brothels—the 17-80s.
Runner up first capital of Vermont, before
The lure of rivers and the manifestly stoneless
Soils of elsewhere.

———

By 2015, Halifax was in eclipse—
The last Dial-up town in America.

Satellite dishes fouled the roofs
Of antique capes and saltboxes, residents
Homesteading for an internet
Fickle as rain.

You would enter a URL into your browser,
Do the dishes, and they'd be dry enough to put away
By the time your page appeared—
No last-minute recipes for that oversize zucchini,
No fritters, eight balls or boats.

Flatlanders from Boston and NY who moved here
For the peace and quiet found
Endless aggravation—washboarding and potholing
Dirt roads to Brattleboro or Shelburne Falls
To update their Facebook, tweet someone,
Or download their mail.

During the icy slide of winter
There was no escape into the Web
Of other people's catastrophes—toilets overflowing

Cruiseships, sharks invading the Outer Banks—
No escape from mud season, when you'd sink in
Eight inches past your axle.

Couples argued
Whose turn it was to circulate
The next broadband petition—
People sold out
Gave up the farm, got what they could
For their bricks and clapboards. People
Got divorced.

II.

Then a cell tower went up
Right at the crossroads.

Those who weathered the Dial-up years—
The hardy few who remained—camped out
To watch spring's leafy unraveling
Obscure the growth of the tower. By July,
We signed up for introductory rates.

Gossip by the mailboxes soon ceased, prayer
Circle in the church basement moved online.
When people found themselves face to face,
They thanked the Almighty
And V-Tel—even the tight-lipped neighbor—
Now practically a saint—who broke ranks
With the historic district and leased
His land for the tower.

We had rejoined America—

Inside, with our digits and thumbs on devices,
Gardens went unpicked and unweeded.
Wood piles waited to be split and stacked,
Fields to be brushhogged. Fall foliage
Blazed and fell
Unnoticed.

We were connected, contented—
Binge streaming Netflix
And cracking
A previously unimaginable cache
Of parental-advisory content.

INCREMENTAL DARKENING

You worry
it's almost over.
I say nothing, not wanting to hear
summer ratcheting down
its own instruments.

Our static serenades
the cows in the front field. Indifferent
tomatoes sag to the ground, burdening us—
zucchini grow into baseball bats
in extra innings.

No time
after work to glean what we can
and go for a kayak. No time
to stop playing the victim. No time
not to hear it anymore.

The heat of the season staggers us.
We agree
to wait until the cold winds
bare the trees, until
the wood is stacked and dried,

until night elbows out the day.

DIVULGENCE

It would be remiss to say
that the world and I
are strangers—

The lemons—on the hills
above *Lago di Garda*—
do they still pucker
in the sun? The winds there
used to prick my eyes
with my own hair—as if to shield me
from a full-on shimmering.
I remember this the way one begins
to speak—and learns to be still. The way
I learned to scratch at love.

I remember this—
and more—but
not how I ended up here.

WELTANSCHAUUNG*

In 1991, I'm retro
short shorts and cuff links,
long hair too curated
for Berlin's no-nonsense scene—
you too are a bit out of it,
but dazzle my world with your planetary eyes
and flowering pants, just ripening into your twenties,
electric and wholesome like the Love Parade.

We meet in German class
With too much in common.
You work in a gallery and fall for knowitalls
at art openings and film premieres—lots of smoke
in Café Hegel but little time to swim in the Wannsee.

I teach English to rough and ruddy Russians
struck by *perestroika*, pried open by *glasnost*,
and stranded in an outpost that no longer exists.

Each morning over *milchkaffee*, our world
gaudy with glamour, we lick our wounds and try on
our *neue weltanschauung* from the night before—
Berlin, all *gemütlich*, unwashed and prickly,
scratches our dreams, tears down self-constructed borders,
and rebuilds the spaces in between. It's a brutal sort of progress—
hard to put our fingers on, akin to liberation,
or growing up.

It feels uncontrollable, irresistible even.
It'll be good for us, we imagine,
turn out alright   in the end.

For all this you are the perfect partner. Underneath your pluck
and bravado, you are a grinning girl of the '70s,
a suburban Brady Buncher—like me—

skirting skinheads and *ausländerfeindlichkeit*
deep in the East, where we're all but squatting.

We were happy, even purposeful then—tropical fish
swimming upstream to explore a grayer
and much cooler world.

At your wedding, years later,
I'll regret to your father
I could not be the one.

* Worldview
 for Lisa

AFTER THE WALL

A boarded up prewar crumbling
with neoclassical flair, packed tight against a pockmarked
pebbly *Neubau* the color of mud,
just off *Käthe-Kollwitzplatz*—the patched up
gut of Berlin's still slumbering East.
At the back end of the third courtyard
up the unlit staircase, beyond the landing
between the 3rd and 4th floors,
past the unheated *Treppenklo* which mostly flushed,
when it wasn't winter,
to the 2-room flat Fülüp renovated
with disheveled *schlank* and limber Stalinesque eyebrows—
somewhat self-mockingly, he called himself
der Fritz.

It was a surprise, when I moved in,
to find the young and the unwashed
showing up at all hours at our door
with a towel.

Unfazed
by the fall of the Wall,
Fritz was goofy and generous,
as was his tub—the only one
for block after block of unrenovated East.
Jammed between sink and stove,
pedestaled across from our table and chairs
under a bare lavender bulb and
a Warhol Marilyn pinup—the bath
was the heart and soul of the *Wohnung.*
A destination, as it turned out—
cleansing an undeodorized world
of coal-dusty ovens and coldwater flats,
one *Ossi* at a time.

Egalitarian Fritz
asked one price for admission—
while you bathed or showered
(there was a handheld attachment)
you had to strut your stuff
(but no curtain)
and put on a show worthy of an audience.

So—
Fritz and I ate our muesli
or drank late night tea while hunky Thorsten
soaked with 18th century Romantics,
in a blue feather boa we had lying around.
Isabel from across the hall—
one child asleep on our floor,
the other back in Cuba—
came by often to cabaret herself clean
in bra and underpants.
          And Vladimir—
who by day removed the rubble
of slug-like apartment houses,
now prime real estate for
Berlin's new skyscrapered soul—
Vlad, drunk on vodka, flung his hair back like Vysotsky
and sang a raspy *Ballad of Childhood*
with a nostalgia not yet common
in those hopeful early days.

At times, more squawk than singing,
a shuffle rather than a dance.
On these occasions
Fritz might shut off the water or call in the *Stasi*.
To each according to his ability, he joked,
helping out-of-it *Ossis*
Wessie up their act.

DUBROVNIK 1990

The old town gathers night
after night on Europe's jagged edge—

unchoreographed, roofless pleasure
laps the slick stone streets—

purse-lipped,
winter-tanned in cold light,
hair dyed, unblinking eyes,
a man sidesteps time,
trapped

in the flow, circling,
not coupled or promenading,
not pausing, statued, to lick another's lips.
Winnowing
for a way in, a way out,

like there's nothing but love
in this look-over-your-shoulder world—
puckered couples stretch out their hands
for what's no longer graspable.

Everything's liminal—
the local *rakija* burns going down.
Evening, as always, continues to circle,
prayer beads in pocket, arm in arm in arms
but his—

It'll be mettle
that matters—in the crush of months ahead.

The hills crowd down
to the splintered sea.
The old walls are crumbling—
companionable as they dare.

IRRECONCILABLE WINTERS*

Saddled with humorless, half-empty
bookshelves and too many sofas—and winter—
alone I heat the New Hampshire house
I bought for two. Shuddered by snow
and record lows, seemingly without end,
my radiators creak and moan as the old furnace
battles hot water through antiquated piping.
My laptop is under siege from CNN.

      In Ukraine, Debaltseve is dammed
      in ice. Streets are gutted from shelling, tenements
      obliterated; what remains is pockmarked
      by rifle fire, bashed in
      and battered, looted. Glass and debris, an occasional
      unexploded grenade, are everywhere hidden
      under snow. A few—the old, infirm, the resolved
      who chose to remain past the latest ceasefire—still walk
      their dogs along deserted, dangersome streets.

Lu, fifteen, no longer willing to pad the icy earth
to do his business, stands on the stoop shivering
in his sweater, until I let him back in to pee
on the rug. The only person I see, with work stormed
into silence, is the plowguy—
grumbling, maligning my too-narrow, nowhere-
to-pile-the-snow driveway. He rips up my lawn then
threatens never to return.

      Ukrainian patriots fight pro-Russian
      Ukrainians and Russians street by street.
      Pensioners bundled in old sheets and rugs
      carry their buckets to be filled at the water truck.
      They barricade themselves in their homes
      without electricity or heat, fearing looters
      as much as shelling and sniper fire.

A cupboard of old clothes, an onion, a half-frozen,
half-rotting cabbage, some mismatched dishes—these
they can never leave unguarded.

I shovel the driveway, pathways and stoops—
even the roof, to keep it from collapsing
on my car. I trudge to the convenience store,
on iced-over sidewalks, to pick up
overpriced, microwavable, eat-by-yourself junk
that weighs me down and leaves me craving.
Newmarket is hunkered down. The streets
belong to the plow trucks. There is nowhere
to go. No one to visit. There is no place safe
to park your car.

The lucky get relocated as the fighting moves
westward. Other families take them in, sharing
the little they have. The displaced bring their few valuables:
Pictures, maybe some jewelry. A few items of clothing.
Beloved animal companions, of course, sometimes
the only family they have left. The fighting burns hot
then recedes, lies dormant for a while, then, like hope,
flares up, again.

Winds whip up overnight, rattling my sleep.
We lose power. I drag my bed, and Lu's,
by the fireplace, which warms only a part of one room,
and bring in the last of the firewood. Trees are down
everywhere—it could take a week, or more,
to repair the lines. I worry the pipes will freeze, my food
will spoil, or get eaten by animals, if I put it out
in the cold. Without thinking, I flush the last
of my water as my cell phone exhausts its charge.
I lose touch with friends, with family,
with the news of the world.

*2015

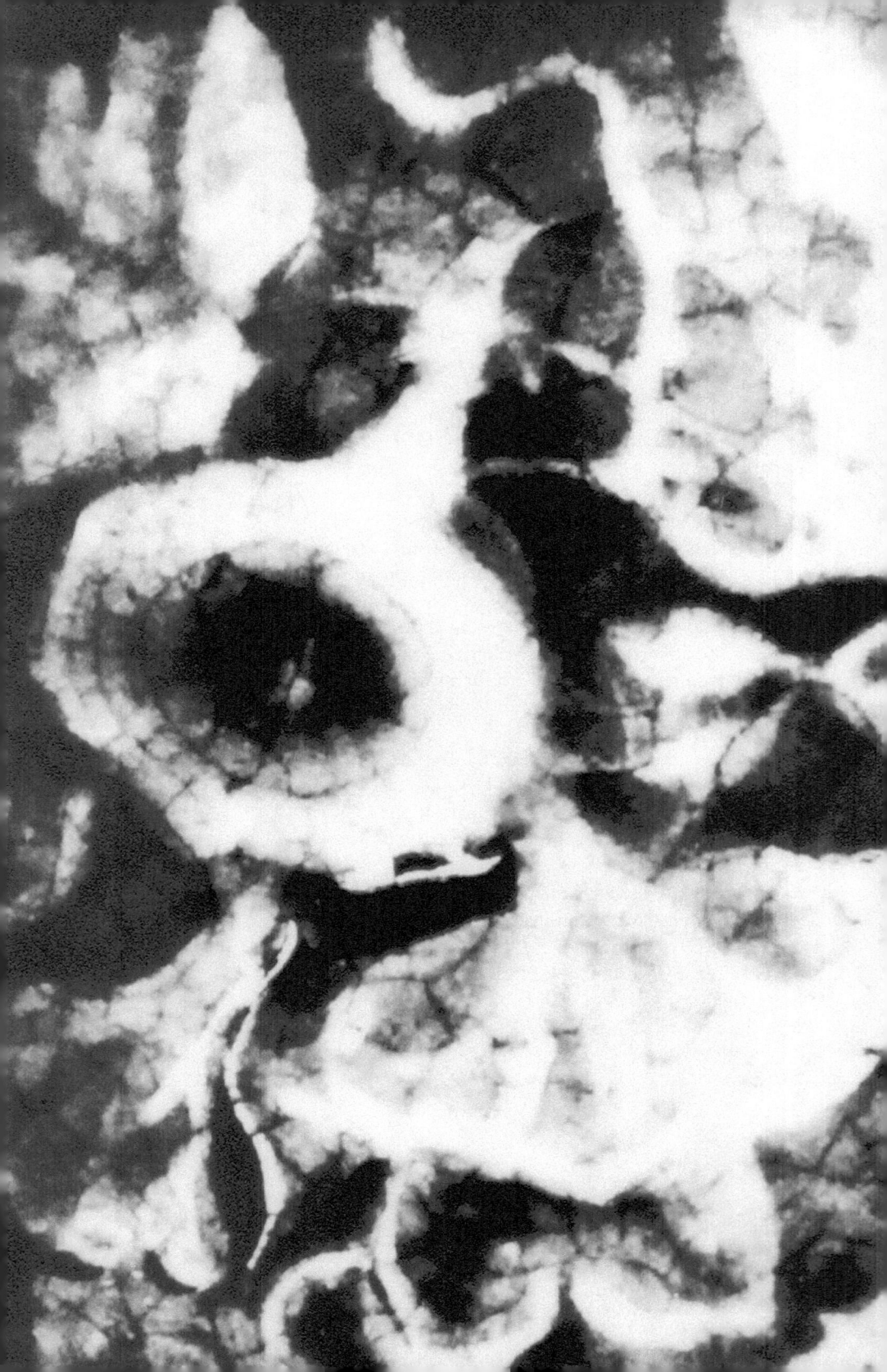

V.

Amor Fati

The wind the chill
a bit of rain—
a respite
from summer's impulsive
arrival—
tyrannous and
before time

The humidity the pollen
you shut the windows
stifling me   us
the rumble
of the dehumidifier
insistent and overwhelming
the birds of morning
the frogs'
evening madness—

Our own brittle cacophony
we call love

SUNSHINE WHEN IT SNOWS*

I am old
But my privilege
I do not
Take for granted.
Middle class and white—
Let's face it, nothing luckier
In this bull-headed world—

Resilient Job's Daughter
I knew enough
To keep a bat by the bed
And jam my door with a chair.
I stood my ground
On a Funk pick-up truck
Slicing silk from the corn.
Life wasn't free
In the land of Lincoln.

Afternoons with Mama
I put out the *Clinton Journal*—
Molten metal
Lead slugs and lino
So loud
I took up the organ—
The only instrument
That could drown out the noise.
Five dollars a funeral and
I found my career—Bach!
What glorious cacophony.

Chickering grand
Platinum and pretty, growing up
I wanted for nothing.
Not five foot two
Best legs in my Illinois yearbook,
But it was brains and grandma got me to college—

Lucky girl in the 1930s, let me tell you.

My shithouse figure
There was no disguising.
So I danced with gay men,
Good grace and safe,
Until I found my mathematician,
My prince—
Seventy-one years we added up
Who could ask for anything more?

My home I own, my income
Is ample, my children are friends
And my friends are fabulous.
Such a privilege
To be alive at 98
or 99—depending
On which of my birth certificates
You believe.

I lace up my shoes
Thirty laps of the living room
Without my walker. Prosecco
In hand —
I still get around.

———

I was run over
In my 80s
By an 18-wheeler.
I have learned
To accept anything
That comes my way.

Not that I suffer Trump lightly
I sleep only four hours a night
And follow the Alternet.
I was for Henry Wallace—
Who else can say that?

My friends today
Thirty or sixty years younger
Waltz with left feet
And go to bed early.

I have had the good fortune
Not to sit out a dance—
Still standing at midnight
Half full my glass.

* for Lynda Copeland

THE TOPOGRAPHY OF BOCA

In Boca Raton,
a grandmother of four emerges
at midmorning, after a low carb evening—
dry as they come Grey Goose martinis, no olives,
no regrets, no water aerobics, not today.

She channels a girl's body—
marred (only slightly) by small purple peonies and climbing clematis.
She's loaded with gold points from bridge club
now that she's laid her tennis racquet down.

> Her mother never played.
> When she wasn't cooking or cleaning,
> she sewed through *Days of Our Lives*
> and *General Hospital* in slippers or sensible shoes.

Grandmother, now Zsa Zsa'd in her 70s,
is (almost) always out on the town—blonded
and teased, powdered and painted—
Never to be seen
without her face on.

This, the topography of Boca—
doctor visits and salons so frequent, there's no time
to grow old.

——

At 86, a grandfather of five
still gets behind the wheel
and his money's worth at the seafood buffet,
but no longer synagogues. Widowed and fully insured,
with an ever-growing portfolio, he is the catch of the day
every day, fetching even a 60-year old price.

37 set-up dinners seated next to available widows,
16 new bridge partners trialed. When finally
go-go grandfather chances upon gold-points grandmother,
takes her measure,
he Crystal Lines her, posthaste, from Stockholm to Antarctica.

Her mother, hemmed in housecoat
and rocking chair, never boarded a plane.

UNSETTLED

Believe me I'd rather
Be down South
Tending sumptuous
Camellia sasanquas
Gorging on satsuma
Straight from the tree
Kayaking along the Moon
with dolphins—
A light shirt and the sun at bay

Hands deep in longleaf pine
Cloaked in Spanish moss
The weeping gauze of cocktail hour
Where vowels in full bloom meet
The spongy consonants of natives—

An overripe kindness
Yaupon holly's restless red greeting—
The gush of strangers
Beauty bush gone to seed

But I'd rather miss
Up North
The great palette change
Generous, companionable green
Holding court for suitors of all colors
Then,
a more spartan kingdom—
The solace of white
and gray

———

Tasting snow sweet on hemlock
Breath you can see
Clear-the-air thinking

Sheets refreshed in the winter wind
A who-needs-coffee wake-up slap
Walking the dogs at dawn

Yes, there will be thick pointillist blurries
Outside crown glass windows
Draped in stiff yellow chintz
Pricks of heat from the fire

And storms!
Phantoms carousing
whirling birling
Across the hilltop

Burying us in blankets
Of scrappy Jack Russells who
Pin down our legs and growl
If we stir, and
Only on cold nights
Condescend to be cuddled

Seek and You Shall Find*

Chickens run backwards in Savannah
at least for Flannery—
A clear view to the Cathedral
from her playpen cage
The latest in better homes
and gardens
Precocious, pigeon-toed
child
of mystery, morals and cheek
Leave me alone or I'll bite you

I seek her again in *Andalusia*—
the home where she found *her* muse
I meet instead a listless
rectangular guide
roused, it seems, to point out
her typewriter
with a disjointed, almost royal
flick—
A fridge twice the price
of a car,
the screened porch, where she humored
farmhands, the curious and the prophets—
Good country people, all

My guide preferred Harry Potter
spoke little and then so softly
I thought he was praying
He left Flannery to my own devices
Near empty bookcases, nameless portraits
ramshackle dairy, suckering
sycamores—He let me photograph him, black eyes
in the shadow of his Ravenclaw cap
crowned from behind by a full fan of blue and green feathers
Peacocks penned where they used to parade

That night
I find her at last on the shoulder
of Highway 26   after a blow out
before I can even make a call—
Tap tap on the window

Good evening Sir...
        Shapeless, haunting, monumental
        in reflective gear and helmet—
        Did I conjure him? Did *she?*
                With lug wrench and tire iron?
...May I be of assistance
I, I—was just calling—
I'm here now
No need waiting

His headlamp shines down
Gamesome eyes
Bulls-eye cheekbones
Zigzag smile—

Are you for real? I ask
Yes Siree
by God I am
I stare up at him
I'm a Road Ranger and I'm here for you—
        Hypnotizing
        Hi-vis reflective raingear
        Full flare of teeth
—And the service is free
He knows
        a cheap skeptic
                when he sees one
And I know
        a good man is hard to find
                in the middle of nowhere

I flash to Flannery and self-preservation
A stroke of good fortune
too good to be true

The Bible salesman who runs off
          with your wooden leg
The guy you flag down for help
who lays waste to your family—

My ranger waits, twirling his wrench
Light catches metal and blurs
in the gleam. I see little stars
and hear: What's the catch?
What's the catch?
          in my staggered mind

I breathe out
Are you my guardian angel?

     Maybe so
Do you have a spare?

* *in homage to Flannery O'Connor*

INTERREGNUM

In streams the sun
bright enough
to fade the sofa
warm enough still
during the day
to remove a layer
or strip down—

       Immobile
I mesmerize
to the unremitting rattle
and whine of the fly's ricochet
in the glory
of leftover light—
hibernating me
till I am one
with the rattle and the sun
prolonging the season—
           bitterer times to come.

As for the fly
trapped between window and storm
too sluggish to find a way in
too cold to back out
       longing
in his vertical vivarium
for inside kin
crawling up the damask curtains
gathering in winter cluster—

He sees

another, curled, legs-up on the sill
a portent of what's to come—soon
the cold will harden the in-between

Life   short
in the scheme of things
as Indian summer
crystallizes in a sigh
              and realigns.

WINTERMISSION

It's dullness disguised as despair—
Endless days of everything
The same hopeless hue

      Where hoarfrost and mirrors
Collide with conscience
         In room after unrelenting room

Here and Now

It's darkening early now
My timing is off

Stars exile
Their own light, hungering
For more distant kin

The evening hard stretches—
Limbering fires and primordial meals

Derelict
Now that you're no longer
Here

I long for
Days chiseled down
A return to that persimmon time

When longing would flicker
Ever so briefly—
Whimpering dogs

At dusk, day lily
Whoop and wham
The hit and run of your smile

Then and there.

Confession

I.

No one is gay
it seems on the Camino de Santiago

Not that I was looking
really
but I must've met a thousand guys
        walking—
Quebecois corporate warriors on leave
geared-up quirky Koreans and
Italians taking their own sweet time
        or bicycling—
spandex and saddlebags speeding by,
wives somewhere behind
        a Don Quixote on horseback even—
What a story to tell the kids!
(adopted, obviously)
…we met as pilgrims
on a spiritual path
        our first kiss in a hermitage
        where Saint Francis—
        then also a pilgrim—
        slept…

What I found, or what found me,
on this camino of otherwise consummate diversity
was one enormous closet
a baroque cache of confidences
gilded and built to endure
an *un*confessional
comprehensive and uncompromising
it walked with me   surrounded me
sheltered me   always
at night   it privated me   fundamentally

after being out for so long

———

I walked five hundred miles
in the closet—
a silent chaperon

II.

By the time I reach Finisterre
I am lighter
in some ways   renewed
Worn out too
at journey's end—
Lame on the shore
where the Apostle's bones were discovered
I embrace the pilgrim ritual
of letting go
finally
setting aflame   with the help of some lighter fluid
what no longer serves

———

I was burning my shoes
when love came for me at last

I had noticed him earlier,
a breathtaking Spaniard
swimming in the waves
with a woman—
his round muscles hummed of surfing and youth
A perfect dark diamond of chest hair
trailed down to low
remarkably
well-fitting shorts

When his salty brown eyes turned towards me
I recoiled   *each time*

as if reproached—
Yet hadn't I dreamt of this man since the Pyrenees
tossing and turning at night
in countless hot, crowded hostels?

After a while
conscious of age and
improbabilities
I limped out of the sea
legs worn out from walking—
crutched and subdued

———

Sheltered by rocks
a Dutch friend and I burn
his long-carried love letters
in the flames of our pilgrim fire
while my boots I burn
for their blistering failures
grateful as I was
that they went the distance

When the man from the surf shows up
I reek of burning leather
rubber and polyester
sandy feet and bulgy calves appear
solid and essential in the softening sun
He says what I've been waiting to hear
my whole life
        (as a pilgrim)
Tienes un cigarillo?

I look up at him
this stunning smiling man
then at my pilgrim friend
accusing me with his stare:
What's this guy doing here?

Oh—

No. I say to my Spaniard
        unexpected as a slap
He stands there
   waiting
my boots threatening
to smother the fire

Seguro? he asks
grasping my gaze
No fumo, I reply
ridiculous   like an apology
he waits
for me
to say something
else   then shrugs
perfect shoulders
turns slowly   eyes in a sigh
and drifts away

III.

My boots smolder
My friend resumes his reading—
I stand there   immobilized
in some kind of trance
until my legs buckle—
I could still make out the dark luster
of his hair at the far end of the beach
and then
he disappears
over the dunes with the sun

I crouch down to revive the fire
as if
nothing had happened
as if
there was nothing else to do

As if
I didn't know God
was a tease

STILL STANDING

I wish to stand tall—
obstinate and unwavering
like mullein
piercing the sky

Thapsus Verbascum
seeding itself blithely
in hardscrabble places
straight-backed in January
no longer ablaze
in summer urgence—yet
undaunted
by wind and ice
and 20 below

Fuck you winter
I will *not* be forgotten!

I do not chitter
like the leftover leaves of a beech
rattling in a crowd
of hangers-on

Nor do I bow to the ground
like boughs of the pine
splintering
at every frozen breath

I gather tight my grayed fur
to guard my weary—
and hold my fraying spear
firm and high
lest you forget
I was here

Gone
gone is my yellow
still—

I am here

Denouement

wonderous winds
lay down the dying day
onto wildflower blankets
pincushioned and poppied

fallen fruit accumulate
helter skelter in the garden
       as if abandoned
       mid-bocce
my rooms I overwhelm
with those I can't possibly consume
       pyramids and doorstops
       grapefruits and pomelos

the heady scent of *zagara*
and desert sands blown across the sea
crowd the blood orange sky
       overheated
groves of half burnt cedar and almond
howl like dogs seeking solace in the night—until
darkness releases a deep exhale
       and sleep or stars
can at last be had

CERAMIC TILE FRAGMENTS, THESE VISUAL POEMS PUNCTUATE MEMORY AS FOUND OBJECTS—ARTIFACTS FROM THE AUTHOR'S TINY EXCAVATIONS AND MEANDERINGS AMIDST THE RUINS, GATHERED LIKE SYLLABLES STREWN ACROSS TIME.

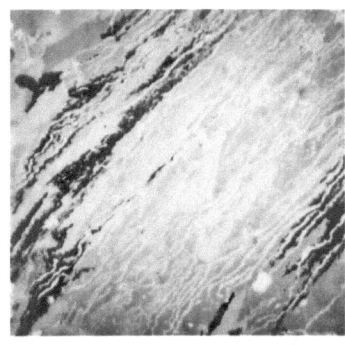 

 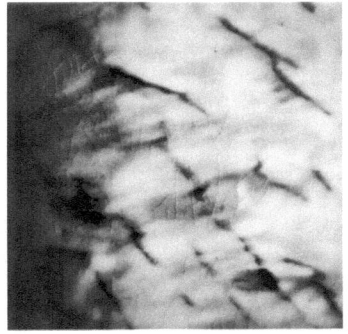

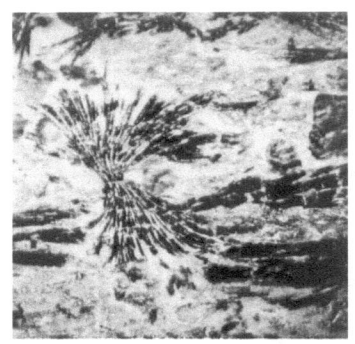 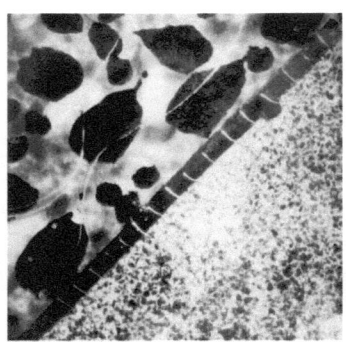

 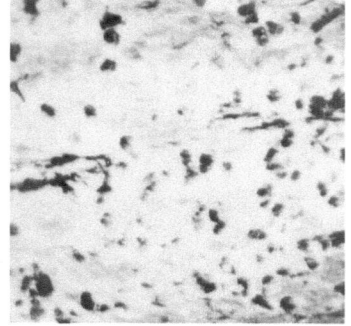

 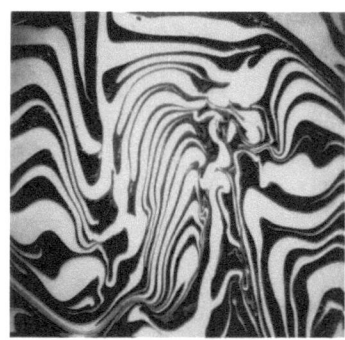

 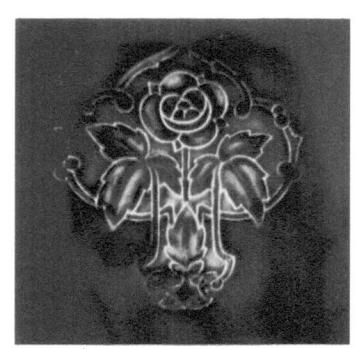

 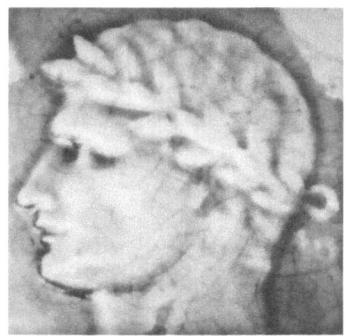

Acknowledgments

I am beyond grateful to my teachers, friends and family who animate my writing and my life. Loving, bounteous thanks to my mom and my partner, David Brewster, my greatest champions, who are at the heart of all my poems. To Lynda and Laurel Copeland I owe the production of this book. I cannot thank them enough for their generous patronage, and for being avid readers and enthusiastic publishers of my poetry in the Halifax, Vermont newsletter. Many thanks to Gwen Davis, John Deziel, Joe Robertson, Antonietta Kies and Mekeel McBride, among my earliest and most spirited readers, and to the reviews and journals at the outermost fringe of the internet, now mostly shuttered, who first published my work and gave me the gumption to carry on writing.

Thank you Decatur Dixon Press, and my editor Lisa Jaye Young, for choosing me as their first living author. This book would not exist but for Lisa's decades of friendship and belief in me, her tireless support and encouragement, her calm in the storm—the weltanschauung we live and share!

To the tumbledown and forsaken places where, over the years, my partner and I rescued treasures from the past (including the glazed terracotta tiles pictured in this book), and to all gardens great and small, you inspire me! Big hugs to my client friends in New England who graciously let me have my way in their perennial beds and borders, and a special thanks to Liz Hull, The Gardener, who generously shared her amazing plant collection and lifetime of knowledge—who mentored me and grew me into the gardener I am today.

Molto grazie to my hosts, Fiona and Diego di San Giuliano. My time gardening on their floriferous Sicilian estate sowed the seeds for several of the poems in this collection. And to Fergus Garrett and the dedicated, soulful gardeners at The Great Dixter, warmest gratitude for sparking my reimaginings of landscape and the act and art of gardening itself.

Thank you Micaela and Frank Boscoe for your hospitality, nourishing the book in its infancy. *Merci* to Jacob Edenfield for the beautiful book design, and Wyn Cooper for sifting through a hundred poems and offering guidance.

ABOUT THE AUTHOR

Gregg Orifici is a poet, memoirist, international educator and garden/
landscape designer. His narrative and lyrical portraits of plants and people
and place weave together documentary realism, social commentary, satire,
and the quiet mystery of the everyday. His experiments with voice, structure
and musicality commingle the intimate with the universal. He has gardened
in residence at The Great Dixter in England, Villa San Giuliano in Sicily, and
Jardín Botánico de Vallarta in Mexico, inspiring his creativity, both on the
page and in the New England gardens he designs. Orifici holds a JD from
Vanderbilt University and an MFA in Creative Writing from University of
New Hampshire. He lives with his artist partner and four Jack Russells on a
hilltop garden-in-progress in southern Vermont.

www.ingramcontent.com/pod-product-compliance
Lightning Source LLC
Chambersburg PA
CBHW031425120626
46545CB00006B/2285